STARTERS

Journeys

Kay Woodward

Text copyright © Kay Woodward 2004

Language consultant: Andrew Burrell
Subject consultant: John Lace
Design: Perry Tate Design
Picture research: Glass Onion Pictures

Published in Great Britain in 2004
by Hodder Wayland, an imprint of
Hodder Children's Books

This paperback edition published in 2008 by Wayland.
Reprinted in 2008 and in 2009 by Wayland, a division of Hachette Children's Books,
an Hachette UK company.
www.hachette.co.uk

The publishers would like to thank the following for allowing us to reproduce their
pictures in this book: Angela Hampton / Family Life Picture Library; 6, 17 (bottom
right), 21 (top) / Corbis; cover, contents page, 4 (top), 5 (top), 7 (top), 9, 10, 11
(bottom), 12, 13, 14, 15, 16 (middle), 17 (top), 18 (top), 19, 20, 21 (bottom), 22 (top),
23 (bottom) / Getty Images; 4 (bottom), 23 (top) / Hodder Wayland Picture Library;
title page, 5 (bottom), 7 (bottom), 8, 11 (top) / Encompass Graphics Ltd; 16 (top and
bottom), 17 (middle) / Zul Mukhida, Chapel Studios; 18 (bottom), 22 (bottom)

A catalogue record for this book is available from the British Library.

ISBN: 978 0 7502 4552 4

Printed and bound in China

Wayland
338 Euston Road, London NW1 3BH

Contents

Going on a journey   4

Near and far   6

Wheels go round   8

Travelling together   10

Along the tracks   12

Up and away   14

Time to pack   16

On the way   18

Getting there   20

Home again!   22

Glossary and index   24

Going on a journey

A journey is when you travel from one place to another. Journeys happen for many reasons.

You might go on a journey to school or to a birthday party.

You might visit friends, or go on holiday to the seaside.

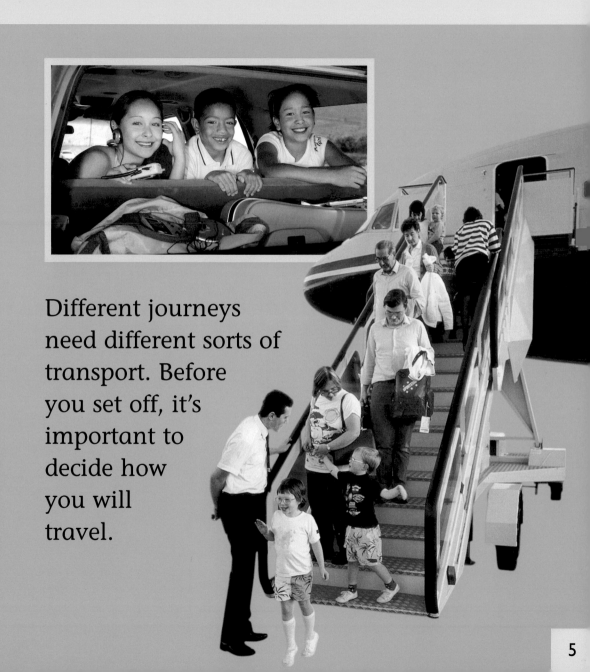

Different journeys need different sorts of transport. Before you set off, it's important to decide how you will travel.

Near and far

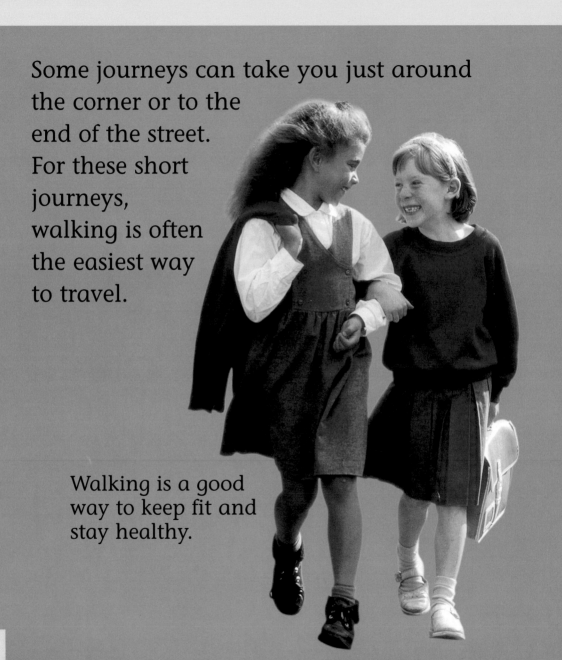

Some journeys can take you just around the corner or to the end of the street. For these short journeys, walking is often the easiest way to travel.

Walking is a good way to keep fit and stay healthy.

Bicycles and scooters
are ideal for longer
journeys – they allow
you to move
more quickly.

Many roads
have cycle paths
beside them,
especially for
bicycle traffic.

Wheels go round

People travel in cars when it is too far to walk or when they want to get somewhere *quickly*.

With a full tank of fuel, a car can travel a long way.

Sometimes a car journey can take a long time, especially when it is holiday season.

When there is too much traffic on the road, cars have to travel very *s l o w l y*.

Travelling together

Buses and coaches can carry lots of people at the same time. A bus makes the same short journey again and again, picking up and dropping off passengers at bus stops along the way.

Passengers wait at bus stops until a bus arrives to pick them up.

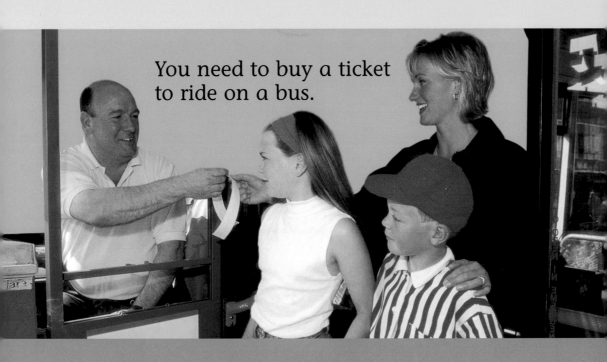

You need to buy a ticket to ride on a bus.

Some coaches have televisions, snacks and toilets on board, to make longer journeys even more relaxing.

716

Along the tracks

Railway trains have lots of carriages. They can carry hundreds of passengers at once.

They **speed** along railway tracks, taking passengers through valleys and tunnels, across bridges and over hills.

In large cities, people travel on underground trains. These can go faster than the cars and buses on the busy roads above.

This train takes people from England to France through a tunnel under the seabed!

Aeroplanes *soar* through the sky, flying quickly over land and sea. They take passengers on journeys all over the world.

Aeroplanes can travel halfway around the world in less than a day!

14

There is only one vehicle that can travel faster than an aeroplane – a spacecraft! Rockets are used to push spacecraft up into the sky until they are **HIGH** above Earth.

Very few people travel by spacecraft now but maybe you will one day!

Time to pack

Once you have decided where to go and how to travel, there is one more decision to make... What should you take on your journey?

A map will help you to find the way.

A tasty snack will keep you going.

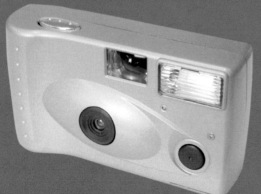

You can use a camera to take pictures of what you see.

If you're going on holiday, you might need cool clothes, sun lotion...

sunglasses...
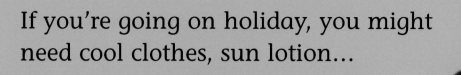

and a hat.

You'll also need a suitcase to pack them in.

On the way

During a journey, there's always something new to look at. One journey might take you past hotels, beaches and  theme parks. Another might carry you past mountains, lakes and castles.

Sometimes, it's time to take a break. Drivers need to rest, people need to go to the toilet and cars need to be filled up with fuel. Passengers might even change to a different sort of transport.

This ferry is carrying cars across the sea.

Getting there

At the end of a journey, it feels good to stretch and yawn. Then, it's time to unpack, look around and have fun!

If you're visiting friends, you can laugh, talk and play together.

At the seaside, you can paddle, swim, build sandcastles and eat ice cream.

In a different country, you might learn about how other people live.

Home again!

Most journeys mean that people travel in two directions – going away and then coming home again.

It's exciting to visit friends and see new places. You might feel sad when it's time to say goodbye.

But, after a long, tiring journey, home is the best place in the world to be!

Glossary and index

Carriage The part of a train where lots of people can sit. **12**

Cycle path A path beside a road or in the countryside that is especially for people riding bicycles. **7**

Fuel A liquid that is burned to make a car's engine work. **8**

Map A small drawing of a town, a country or the world. **16**

Passenger A person who travels in a vehicle but is not the driver. **10, 12, 14, 19**

Seabed The ground at the bottom of the sea. **13**

Spacecraft A vehicle used for travelling in space. **15**

Traffic Vehicles travelling along the road. **9**

Transport Vehicles that can move people and things from one place to another. **5**